Gullible

The Perfect Guidebook About Gullibility for People Gullible or Not.

Phil Hugh

gul·li·ble
adjective
easily persuaded to believe
something; credulous.
"an attempt to persuade a
gullible public to spend their money"

Table of Contents

Introduction: Are We Living in a Gullible World?

"Teddy said it was a hat, so I put it on. Now dad is saying, "where the heck's the toilet plunger gone?"
Shel Silverstein

The thing about people, especially when you always mean what you say, is that you assume everyone else is the same. It's human nature to always see the good in others, and sometimes this causes some of us to be exploited by a fraudster, who will take advantage of our good nature.
We are all gullible to some extent but let us try not to be too gullible and easily fooled.

What is Gullibility and Why Are People Gullible?

A gullible person is someone who is easily manipulated or tricked. Usually it is an indication of a failure in social intelligence. Gullibility is closely related to credulity, which is the willingness of someone to believe anything, even without evidence. This is also closely related to a phenomenon known as a Confirmation Bias. And a whole book can be written on this subject, but for now, just know that we all are influenced by our biases. We all have inclinations or prejudices for or against something. These are often built up over many years, including the way we have been are brought up. It is not necessarily bad, but we do need to reflect on this often enough so as not to be easily fooled. But gullibility and Confirmation Bias often go hand in hand and can make a person quite easy to fool and manipulate into believing something that is not at all real. That is because the person is already inclined in a certain way, and a skillful fraudster can make use of this inclination to his advantage. So, one ought to be mindful of this.

According to the psychologist, Daniel Kahnean, people tend to process information through two systems:

System 1—Fast Thinking. The automatic and intuitive kind of thinking.

System 2—Slow Thinking. The rational, analytical, and effortful kind of thinking that demands thorough evaluation of any information.

Why People Believe Easily

System 1 is the built-in mechanism by which most people function. When information is fed to anyone, he will deal with this automatically, because trust is second nature to any human being. Gullibility becomes an issue when System 1 is automatically switched on when instead System 2 is required of the situation. For this to happen alarm bells have to go off as when it is "too good or you are surprised ". Slow down and take stock of the situation. Maybe trusting your instinct and common sense, is the way to go.

Why someone is more gullible than others may be related to several things:

1. **Personality.** Believe it or not, some people are just simply harder to break than others, and this is usually due to their core. Some people are just made tougher than others, so they are hard to get through. But some people are flimsy, and they do not know how to say "NO". Which one do you want to be?

2. **Present mood.** Your present mood can affect how susceptible you are to be falling into traps. Someone who is in a positive mood will activate System 1 of thinking, while another who is in a bad mood will be more doubtful and therefore, careful and attentive. Be conscious of what mood you are in.

3. **The current state of being.** More than present mood, one's gullibility may also be influence by one's current state of being. A person who is exhausted from work or

who is severely inebriated will be easier to work on, than someone who is completely attentive. The same can be said for a person who is giddy with love or emotionally distracted.

4. **Past experiences**. Trust is an innate character and it is meant to exist throughout life, unless a bad experience disrupts your belief. Someone who has dealt with deception will most likely be more cautious than others. However, don't be an overboard skeptic. A good balance is required. There are times you will just have to forgive and forget, and that's for your happiness.

5. **Past hardships** Contrary to the thinking that "what doesn't kill you, makes you stronger", studies have shown that people who have suffered from bullying, major illnesses, family trauma, and other difficulties, become susceptible to peer pressure because they do not trust their own judgment. This is where your mental strength should come to the fore. You can just think back to when this has happened to you and accept that it has, and move on. Practice in your mind to counter it. The more you practice the better.

6. **Educational attainment.** One's intelligence and in-depth knowledge can also affect his gullibility. Someone who is completely clueless about something will be quick to believe anything; whereas someone well-informed will not be quick to trust things easily. Maybe you should not believe it first, and make a mental note to check it out.

In general, every person is born with a gullible nature because innocence does not know the difference between right and wrong, so trust is automatic. But even children do not remain gullible all the time. As early as five years old, children have been known to show skepticism that they may or may not carry on for the rest of their lives.

Skepticism may seem negative at first glance, but you have to understand that it is protective in nature. There are many foolish things that should not escape your power of observation.

Maybe you have lost money many times, due to investment scams that only sound good, but do not deliver. Maybe you always find yourself, at the other end of an elaborate prank, and everyone is rolling on the floor, laughing. You know what they say, "fool me once, shame on you; but fool me twice…" Do you really have to be fooled twice, thrice or more times? This book is going to open your eyes and make you more alert and self-assured.

Chapter 1: Gullibility in History

Anyone, smart or not, can become gullible sometimes. That only goes to show that you are not alone with this. As a matter of fact, there are a number of events and people in history, that have displayed some level of gullibility.

Stories in History Where People Were Fooled

Countless stories traveled through history that changed and unnerved how people thought about life. The following are some of the most significant:

The Trojan Horse
The Trojan horse is a humongous wooden statue of a horse built by the Greeks. After the 10-year siege, they sailed away, leaving the Trojan horse with a few men inside, including Odysseus. Now, as the Greeks sailed away, the Trojans pulled the large structure into their city.

That night, the hidden force came out of the wooden statue, and they let the rest of the Greek forces through the gates. This maneuver finally ended the war and left the city of Troy in utter ruin.

The Trojans were too overjoyed, drunk with the thought of their victory. They became vulnerable and let their guard down.

The Piltdown Man

Found in Piltdown, East Sussex in 1912, what was thought to be the remains of an early species of man. It was phenomenally thought to be the missing links in the history of evolution, as theorized by Charles Darwin. But unfortunately, this worldwide attempt to deceive was found out because apparently, the bones were of a modern man, but his lower jaw was replaced by that of an orangutan.

The entire human race probably celebrated the discovery of this deception because who would want to have orangutan ancestors, right?

Anna Anderson as Anastasia

The massacre of the entire Romanov Family during the Russian Revolution ensured the eradication of any legitimate heir to the throne. Soon after, however, rumors had spread that some members of the family were able to escape.

In 1920, a certain Anna Anderson surfaced along with so many other claimants. Following an attempt to end her life, she confessed that she was Princess Anastasia and for decades, she tried to claim her royal inheritance. And who wouldn't try? But while many of the people did not believe her claim, she had a huge following. Unfortunately, a DNA test performed posthumously confirmed that she is not related to the Romanov's and is, actually Franziska Schanzkowska.

People do want to believe in fairy tales. Are you one?

War of the Worlds Radio Broadcast

Orson Welles did not really intend to deceive anyone, but his efforts surely deceived a lot of people. Using H.G. Well's novel, The War of the Worlds, Welles sent out fake radio bulletins that described an alien invasion in New Jersey.

It was quite creative, but many listeners did not catch up as they should and thought that a real invasion was happening. It caused a mass hysteria—involving suicides, stampedes, and angry demonstrations. But was it innocent or did Welles intended to cause panic? Well, he will always be "the Man from Mars", at least.

Lies Becoming Truth

It was Hitler who said "If you use a lie so "colossal" it will be believed, because no one "could have the impudence to distort the truth so infamously". And it was his Minister of Propaganda, Joseph Goebbels, who said: "If you tell a lie big enough and keep repeating it, people will eventually come to believe it".

In this modern-day, there are hyperlinks on the internet where deception is used in messaging campaigns and microtargeting. With convincing slogans that are engagingly repetitive, they are no doubt very effective. Criminals often rely on you to be lazy and not fact check before believing what you were led to see. Just know that what you were directed to see on the internet is almost always slanted towards a questionable scheme or a downright wrong idea. Usually, it is prudent to never click on any link unless you are absolutely sure it is safe. If you are not sure, do not click. As far as the internet is concerned, curiosity can kill you.

The truth is that people will believe anything, as long as it makes sense to them even if it is only to them and no one else. Much more so if it will make things more convenient. Again, do not be foolishly lazy.

Famous People Who Were Found Gullible

If you are worried that you have been gullible a few times, understand that it can happen to anyone. It even happens to famous people, so no one is safe from this:

Alanis Morisette. The famous singer-songwriter, who wrote the song "Oughta Know" did not know better when she lost as much as $4.8 million to her business manager, Jonathan Schwartz. She said that her trust in people was "shaken to the core". The amount was stolen over the course of seven years. No red flag? He claimed an addition to gambling as his defense, which was, of course, struck down. Alanis should have noticed his fondness for gambling as a glaring red flag. Generally speaking, watch out for expensive habits in people handling your money.

Anne Hathaway. This wonderful actress lost over $2.4 million to her ex-boyfriend. Raffaello Follieri, who posed as someone from the Vatican, selling properties in Italy. Could this be a case of love euphoric buzz?

Dane Cook. The thing about the most successful scams is that they are performed by people who know you. You wouldn't have been scammed if you did not trust too much, right? Well, that's what happened to Dane Cook, when his brother stole as much as $12 million from him, through the years that he was working as Dane's manager. Often times a person starts out with good intentions. Over time a trust was built and Dane was not paying attention.

Kiefer Sutherland. He may have been the President in Designated Survivor but lost as much as $869,000 to what he thought was going to be a profitable cattle business. Unfortunately, the con artist, Michael Wayne Carr never invested Sutherland's money. The lesson here is that one should not be lazy when a large amount of money is involved, and not be too trusting. Money is often difficult to resist.

LeAnn Rimes. When people suddenly get fame and fortune, problems tend to follow. After her hit album, she found out that her father and co-manager, stole as much as $7 million from her earnings. This resulted in an ugly family battle. Unfortunately, members of family stealing from each other is not infrequent, since eyes are often shut because "it's family".

Liv Tyler. Steven Tyler's daughter trusted her beauty consultant too much. Maria Gabriella Perez stole as much as $214,000 when she stole Tyler's credit card details. She was also Jennifer Aniston's ex-beautician, and the actor said she was not surprised by her actions. So, there must have been warning signs which were ignored by Liv.

Robert De Niro. De Niro may be a famous gangster in movies, but he wasn't as tough when the art dealer, Lawrence Salander sold one of his paintings, behind his back. He reportedly lost as much as $1 million for this artwork. The actor said at first he did not pay much attention, but then started noticing how Salander was flying around in private jets. Alarm bells going off in his head probably saved him many dollars.

Sting. The former Police, lead-singer's longtime financial adviser Keith Moore, a chartered accountant, was jailed six years for having stolen a reported $9.5 million from 1988 to 1992. It transpired that Sting had about 100 bank accounts and maintaining close attention to them was left to Keith Moore. Maybe the temptation was just too strong. Perhaps having so many bank accounts is somewhat gullible.

Tiger Woods. He may be a badass on the golf course, but the famous golfer became a victim of identity theft and was billed as much as $17,000 in the span of two years. Of course, he is far from being the only one. Kim Kardashian, Will Smith, Steven Spielberg, Oprah Winfrey, to name a few. In fact they can be easy targets, being famous with lots of public information out there. Anyone can call American Express claiming to be Tiger, giving his personal information, and asking for a replacement card to a changed address. There are various ways you can be tricked into divulging your personal information and a few chapters can be written on this subject. It would be a good idea to familiarize yourself with the many techniques used by identity thieves, by asking Google.

Gullibility in Literature

The world has noted various evidence of gullibility throughout history. Even books have depicted gullibility in different forms. The following are some of the most famous tales you have probably read before:

The Adventures of Pinocchio. Everyone knows Pinocchio's story. He is a wooden boy, made by Geppetto, whom a fairy breathed life into. He was most famous for his elongating nose, but his adventures involved being lured into doing countless forbidden things, often more than once by the same impish rogues. This led the little wooden boy into a cage as Stromboli's prisoner, then to the road to Pleasure Island where he learned to smoke, drink, and gamble, and finally the little boy was transformed into a donkey.

Little Red Riding Hood. This famous tale about a girl with a lovely red coat, who encounters a sneaky wolf on her way to her grandmother's house. Gullible and naïve, she carelessly reveals her destination to the dangerous wolf, who then poses as her grandmother being ill in bed. This is a tale one ought to learn by heart so that in real life you may recognize who is the wolf in grandma's clothing.

The Emperor's New Clothes. In this tale, the Emperor employs two weavers to tailor for a new suit, for a parade that was scheduled to happen. But instead of actually creating a suit, they merely pretended to make one. They fooled the emperor into believing that his new clothes will appear invisible to anyone who is unfit or incompetent. So even though his ministers and others could see that he was wearing nothing, they all pretended to see the nonexistence clothes for fear of appearing stupid. The Emperor paraded his new clothes, and everyone had to watch, until a little boy finally screamed that the emperor was buck naked. When you have too much to lose you might go along with the ridiculous, but be wary of the little child.

Genesis: The Story of Adam and Eve. This final example of tales is from the Bible. This story follows that of Creation after God created the first Man and Woman. Adam and Eve were brought to the Garden of Eden, and they were told to enjoy everything they could find except for the fruit of the Tree of Knowledge. One day, Eve encountered a serpent that told her she could eat the forbidden fruit and become like God. Not only did she believed it for herself, but she also lured Adam to do the same. Immediately after partaking of the fruit, both their eyes were open, and they became ashamed of not wearing any clothes. When God returned to the garden and was looking for them, they hid from him, embarrassed that they were naked. This, as we all know, led to their banishment from the Garden of Eden and marked the fall of mankind.

There are times when the consequences of gullibility are dire to the extreme. Gullible Presidents or Prime Ministers can cause untold miseries. President Carter said that since the end of the Second World the USA has fought, or still fighting, over 240 wars, to no good outcome. The USA is a gullible nation, perhaps? https://www.amazon.com/Gullible-Superpower-Support-Democratic-Movements/dp/194442492X/ref=sr_1_1?keywords=gullible+superpower&qid=1583232418&sr=8-1
Stories of gullibility date back to the beginning of man, and everyday people continue to deal with this because people won't stop manipulating people, and there will be those who will always fall into the traps. Whether you are that person or not, you may still find this book useful and ought to continue reading.

Chapter 2: Fake News and Conspiracy Theories

As evidenced from the previous chapter, anyone can be deceived. If the mighty Trojans can lose in war by pure deception, surely any plain Jane can fall into the same traps. In this modern world, where information is but a click away, fake news has become a banality, to say the least.

It does not choose its victims but spreads itself like a spider web, ready and waiting. You do not have to be foolish to take a glance at a conspiracy theory or consider the plausibility of fake news. You just happen to be passing by. The deception involved is elaborate and almost hard to avoid. This calls for a healthy dose of skepticism kicking in, and asking the following questions:

- Does the information come from a credible source?

- How many people believe this?

- Is there available evidence to support this?

- Does it coincide with your core beliefs?

- Is the story too captivating?

If a story fits into your way of thinking, was shared by someone credible, and was believed by the majority, surely all the evidence being presented cannot be dismissed. And if it tells a good enough story, it should be real, right? Maybe.

The Most Famous Conspiracy Theories

Maybe these people are bored or maybe they just have wild imaginations. Some of these conspiracy theories rocked the world, and are still keeping eyebrows raised, all over.

Paul McCartney is Dead.
Supposedly, Paul McCartney of the Beatles had died tragically in a car accident and was sneakily replaced by a look-alike throughout the remainder of their career. According to theorists the album cover of Abbey Road symbolizes some kind of funeral procession in his name, and in the image, John Lennon stands as a clergyman in all white, George Harrison is a grave digger dressed in denim, Ringo Starr is a mourner dressed in black, while the person who is standing for Paul McCartney is walking without his shoes on.
This conspiracy theory grew so big that believers thought the information of McCartney's death had been embedded in their songs. John Lennon was said to have sung "I buried Paul" in the song "Strawberry Fields Forever".

The Assassination of John F Kennedy
Regarded as the "mother of all conspiracies", there are about 1000 books written about this controversial death. Each version had a different narrative. Could the assassination be the work of the CIA or the Mafia? Some even said that it could be the work of the KGB, or Fidel Castro of Cuba, and even his Vice President Lyndon Johnson.

But on November 22, 1963, JFK was shot dead by two bullets. The 1964 Commission on the Assassination of President Kennedy, the Warren Commission, concluded after 10 months of deliberation, that Lee Harvey Oswald acted alone. It also concluded that Oswald's death 48 hours later shot by a local nightclub owner Jack Ruby was an act of impulsive revenge. Over the next few years, critics turned public opinion against the report. Indeed, compelling evidence was uncovered casting reasonable doubt on the report. Were members of the Warren Commission dishonest or gullible?

Jesus and the Bible
There are countless conspiracy theories about the Bible, but the most significant of the many tales spun about it was started by the book, "The Holy Blood and the Holy Grail". The theorists believe that Mary Magdalene was Jesus' lover, and during their time together, they had children.
This theory was given life in a Dan Brown's novel made into a movie. The Da Vinci Code, starring Tom Hanks, attracted the attention of many, who had to pause for a while to see if any of it were real. Isn't this just Hollywood entertainment?

The Earth is Flat
During ancient times, before world explorations, most believed that the Earth was flat; and that at some point you would arrive at the edge of the world. Today, some gullible people still believe in a flat Earth. Unfortunately, even with countless evidence, modern science and orbiting satellites, it is no use convincing Members of the Flat Earth Society of their folly. Instead, they believe in a "round Earth conspiracy" perpetrated by NASA. One would think their membership is on the decline as a result of more education, but instead, it is rising at the rate of about 200 a year, mostly Americans and Britons. Do they really believe, or are there faking it?
Vaccinations

Vaccines have proven to be one of the greatest health success stories. Once upon a time (and even until this day), there are people who do not trust vaccines. Conspiracy theories have led to massive anti-vaccine movements. Diseases such as measles, smallpox, polio which killed millions, were all but conquered by vaccines, have now reappeared. The fact that infectious diseases have been a major factor in shaping the history of mankind, make the anti-vaccine movements extremely dangerous. That gullibility can change the course of history is no exaggeration.

Elvis is Alive

On August 16, 1977, Elvis was found dead from cardiac arrhythmia, and conspiracy theorists understand that no one can possibly die of a simple heart irregularity, right? Followers of this story became known as "Alivers" and they had various shreds of evidence to support their claims including:

- the 50-year seal on the autopsy

- the misspelled name of Elvis on his tombstone. It says Aaron, when it should say Aron.

- his insurance that was never claimed

- the many Elvis sightings

Theorists believe that Elvis faked his death because he had to go under witness protection, working for the FBI.

UFO (Unidentified Flying Objects)

Many of us have no idea of the vastness of the Universe of countless billions upon billions of stars. To say that there are as many stars as grains of sand on earth is not an exaggeration. There are as many stars as grains of sand on earth. Think about that. But space is mostly emptiness and the nearest star, Proxima Centauri, is 4.24 light-years away, almost certainly an impossible distance for a living being to travel. To assume that the vast universe has intelligent life other than us is not necessarily gullible because the chances are there. But the countless explorations have not brought anything credible, despite the numerous UFO sightings all over the world. Theorist believes that the government has been working hard to cover up the existence of aliens with real-life MIB suppressing people into silence. Many do believe in science fiction.

HIV and AIDS

When AIDS (Acquired Immunodeficiency Syndrome) was first announced to the world, it shocked everyone. It was frightening and deaths were piling up, but eventually, people learned that the source of AIDS is HIV and it can be contracted through sexual intercourse and needles. Why it was affecting mostly gay men and minority groups, became clear in the future, but conspiracy theorists believed that AIDS was a product of the CIA, so that they may control the population of these specific kinds of people. This is naïve, but so is calling HIV "AIDS" since this made a perfectly good word into one that is bad. Do we not miss using "aids" as something good? Same thing with "gay". This is everyday Gullibility.

9/11 Attack

Since 2001, September 11 (9/11) will always be known as the infamous day, when the Twin Towers of the World Trade Center were attacked by Islamic Terrorists. Many of us watched in horror on televisions as the Towers came crushing down into piles of rubble. Al-Qaeda claimed responsibility, and that was later proved beyond a reasonable doubt by all credible intelligence agencies. But conspiracy theorist suggests that the fall of the twin towers was due to controlled demolitions, a plot by the CIA, US Government or Israel. The objective? To pave the way for the Invasion of Iraq. Whether the US Government is truly insane to manage such a catastrophe, the world only has a memorial to remind them of the wonder that used to be the twin towers.

Is Al-Qaeda gullible, to take on a super superpower like the United States? By carrying out such an elaborate attack, the United States is given a good excuse to invade Afghanistan and then Iraq. Any winners, history will decide.

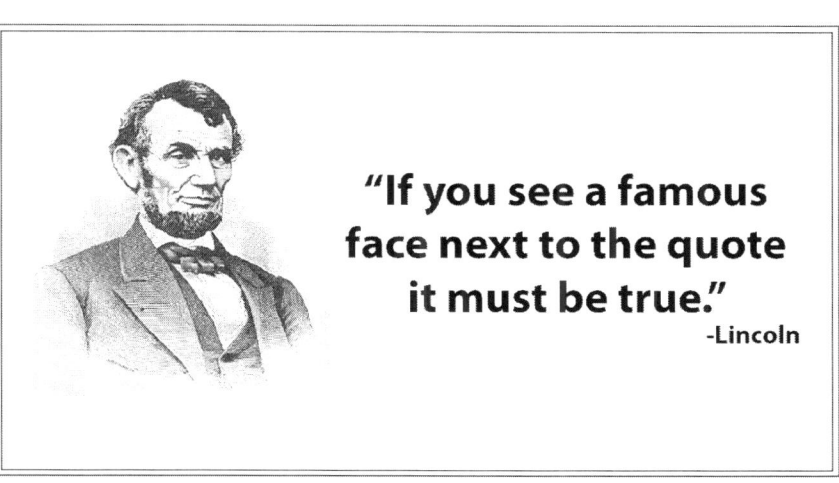

How to Spot Fake News

Fake news has been around for as long as there has been paper, but nowadays people are so swamped by an enormous collection of fake news, it is quite hard to distinguish truth from false. In the past, if you want to see juicy news, you go to the tabloids. Today you see all kinds of sensational news on so-called reputable papers.

Investigation and discernment, in this day and age, is somewhat more problematic. When you see the news, no matter what paper you are looking at, you need to be able to tell if it is fake or not. Here are some guidelines you can follow:

1. **Verify the source.** Where is the information coming from? Is it one person, a company or a group? Explore the framework of the source. Check its mission and vision and verify their contact information. It is much like shopping. You want to get your information from a credible source.

2. **Read beyond the headlines.** Headline baiting is quite common nowadays. To bait people with juicy information, they will headline something enticing that may be far from the truth. So, before you accept the headline as true, you might want to read the entire, or at least most of, the article first.

3. **Investigate the author.** Find out who wrote the piece, and try to find out more about this person. Find out about his background, his affiliation, and so forth. Is this person real? Is he credible? Does he have the tendency to show some bias?

4. **Check the resources provided in the text.** If there are sources quoted within the text, study each one of them and make sure that they are credible.

5. **Is it a joke or a satire?** Some pieces may be intended as a joke or satire. If it seems too much, maybe it was exaggerated for entertainment purposes only. Do not get riled on about anything you see for the first time, without making sure of its content.

6. **Check the date.** Information in the news is only relevant if it is current. News about an earthquake that has happened a decade ago shouldn't cause people to panic, because it's already happened. So before panicking, check the date the article was published.

7. **Carry out your own fact-check.** If there isn't enough information for you to work with, then you should go after the evidence yourself. You can also ask an expert. Consult someone who knows more about the topic. Google itself is a great place to fact check.

8. **Are you biased?** Do you think your inclinations are causing you to be a little gullible? If the information is going to support something you already believe in, you could let your guard down. Check your sentiments. Making sure that you are still treating the information as if you are on the other side of the news, looking in, might not be a bad idea.

Chapter 3: The Pitfalls of Gullibility

The most magnificent display of gullibility happens every 1st of April, on a day called April Fools' Day. While the origin of this day is not clear, what we can be sure of is that on this day, all kinds of pranks are performed with many becoming victims.

Gullibility in the Face of Practical Jokes: Funny April Fools Jokes
Also known as All Fool's Day, on this day every year, the world prepares the most elaborate prank, and these are some of the most significant ones carried out in history:

1. **The Swiss Spaghetti Harvest.** In 1957 the BCC announced that there is a heavy spaghetti crop growing in Switzerland, and a harvesting is happening. The broadcast showed people plucking noodles from trees and everyone wanted to get some for themselves. Of course, it was all a hoax, but who wouldn't believe it? It was on BBC Television.

2. **Temporary Decrease of Gravity.** In 1976, the BBC announced through an English astronomer, Patrick Moore, that there will be a temporary alignment of the planets Pluto and Jupiter. This so-called alignment will cause gravity to decrease a little, and the network received countless calls confirming what they had supposedly felt. One caller said that she witnessed her

friends lifting from their chairs and floating slightly in the sitting room. Beware of the power of suggestion.

3. **Modernizing the Big Ben.** In 1980 the BBC (yet again) announced that the iconic Big Ben was going to get a modern refurbishment to welcome the digital era, but this caused such an uproar that they had to quickly apologize for the joke.

4. **Virgin UFO.** To better fool the people, Richard Branson of the Virgin Group, carried out his prank on March 31 instead of April the first. In 1989 a sighting of some kind of spaceship was found, and when the cops arrived, a spaceman in a silver suit emerged from the ship. But little did they know, it was Richard Branson disguised as the spaceman, and this was not a ship from space at all.

5. **The Space Needle is Down.** The famous Seattle Space Needle has represented Seattle for so long, so in 1989 when news came out that it had fallen, everyone was shocked. The show that aired the prank received as much as 700 callers expressing massive horror for their loss. That's 700 who bother to call, surely, many more thousands believed.

6. **Nixon is running again.** In 1992, President Richard Nixon announced his bid for re-election in a radio broadcast. This brought disappointment and outrage to the people who felt threatened with the news, only to find out that it wasn't Nixon at all but a prank.

7. **The Taco Liberty Bell.** In 1995, Taco Bell announced that they would be buying the Liberty Bell. This ad campaign wasn't accepted with glee. The effort, however, changed the way companies dealt with April Fools. They realized they could use it as a great opportunity and a precedent was established.

8. **The Left-Handed Whopper.** In 1998, a full-page ad appeared in USA Today introducing Burger King's "left-handed Whopper". They said that they recognized the neglect of the left-handed population, so they created this variety to be more inclusive. Now, this prank was a success because people headed to Burger King and started ordering left-handed or right-handed Whoppers. What kind of Whopper would you have ordered in 1998?

9. **The Invisible Wonder Woman Jet.** In 2010, Hot Wheels released the Invisible Wonder Woman Jet which was nothing but an empty plastic box. This amazing idea was such a hit that they were selling like hotcakes, essentially transparent empty packages labeled "Wonder Woman Invisible Jet".

10. **Why Doesn't America Read Anymore?** In 2014, the National Public Radio (NPR) proved an amazing point by posting an article with the title, "Why Doesn't America Read Anymore?" Quick to come on the defensive were those who said, "Of course we read" or "I read all the time". But clearly, they weren't reading because if they had read beyond the headline and clicked the link, they will be taken to the post: "genuine

readers". There it goes on to talk about the fact that some people never go beyond the headline, and then it gave a clear instruction to NOT COMMENT after reading this. The funniest part of this prank is not that some people proved the point NPR was making, but that they left follow-up comments to explain why they commented, in the first place.

Famous Con Artists and Their Most Elaborate Cons

Now pranks are funny once everything has been revealed, but a con is a different thing. Some cons can be very immoral, and you would wonder how someone could do such a thing.

Charles Ponzi and the Infamous Ponzi Scheme
The Ponzi Scheme will always be attributed to the one person who cheated people into an investment that never achieve the returns that it promised. He became known as one of the greatest swindlers in history. He convinced people to invest in his coupon business. And with his charisma, at one point he was making as much as $250,000 every day. He was such a good a con artist, that some people were still investing, even when he was detained in prison.

Frank Abagnale
Have you seen the movie, "Catch Me If You Can?" Frank Abagnale became quite famous for scamming his way through almost anything. He faked his way to becoming a lawyer, professor, doctor, and pilot. When he was in prison, he even convinced the guards that he was an undercover prison inspector, and he was sent there to speak with a contact. His brilliant talent for counterfeiting eventually led him to become a consultant to the FBI.

Bernie Madoff

For concocting a con that allowed him to bag as much as $64.9 Billion, he was truly one of the most successful con artists, until he was caught in 2008 after running the scam for 30 years. His elaborate con put him at the pinnacle of Wall Street. For 3 decades he prospered, and he was very generous to everyone around him. There were red flags raised by a few investigators who did the math on his methods of investment and maintained that it did not add up. However, his reputation was so strong that the authorities took his side. There was a saying "you can doubt God, but not Bernie". Does this remind you of "If you use a lie so "colossal" it will be believed"?

P.T. Barnum

Phineas Taylor Barnum was a con artist, prankster, and fraud. He was the Greatest Showman, but his critics called him a swindler and a cheat, with his bearded lady and her bearded baby. He claimed to be a showman: "See a real Mermaid, tickets selling fast". Despite his notoriety, he was invited to the Buckingham Palace by the Queen and then to the White House. He coined the phrase "There's a sucker born every minute." The con man has no respect for his victims.

Televangelist Jesse Duplantis

Televangelist Jesse Duplantis wants his followers to pray and "believe for" a new 4th private jet for him. And then to chip in for a Dassault Falcon 7X saying that if Jesus is alive today, He would not be riding a donkey. His other 3 jets were of not sufficient range and he needed to fly non-stop to every place in the United States to preach God's words. Jets will get him nearer to God, he said, and his followers believe in him, he also said. There are hundreds of televangelists and radio evangelists who are enormously successful monetarily, and flying around in their own private jets is not uncommon, to do God's work more efficiently, so they say. Their followers believe that donating to their billionaire lifestyle is contributing to God, and they will be blessed a hundredfold in return. Lost in translation is that the disparity between a donkey and a jet plane is all of transportation ever invented. Also lost is the fact that Jesus was practicing humility, riding a donkey instead of a horse. One televangelist, on why a private jet is essential, said in a YouTube video that he could not pray in a commercial airline while sitting with rows upon rows of demons, his fellow passengers. Why are televangelists so successful financially? They cater to some mighty deep-rooted yearning of their followers, and satisfying that need is obviously, extremely profitable. https://www.youtube.com/watch?v=PhSn3tDIYZc.

How to Spot a Con Man and Why Do People Fall for Such Traps?

Whether you're talking about cons, pranks or even fake news, the truth is that people fall for such traps because they allow themselves to be fooled. But why do these things really happen?

- The most important thing you need to realize about cons is they are after the big picture, so to make sure you stay for that, they will keep you interested. They do this by letting you win some. If this is an investment scam, you will enjoy some profit, and it will feel so good — so you will invest more and then things will go downhill.

- Con artists will call you by your name, and you immediately think they can be trusted. They make it personal and can even pretend to be someone you knew from before. You believe it because they will have learned what it takes to convince you—and this sense of familiarity is going to distract you.

- Some people are more vulnerable than others and con artists can spot these vulnerabilities, and use them as targets. Con artists use another person's emotions to their advantage. And when they find an opening, they will make their move. And while on the subject of vulnerability, con artists will make themselves appealing by offering to show some vulnerability or flaw. People tend to trust those who do not appear threatening. So, a good con man will reveal certain faults, anxieties, and they will ostensibly open up their heart so that you can trust them.

- Con artists know how to get you talking. The people who get conned are the ones who do not ask a lot of questions. They instead, answer countless questions and give much of themselves away. To be able to hook someone, a con artist will bait you through your passions and don't forget, your confirmation biases as well. You gave away your heart when you talk unmindfully.

- Mirroring is the act of copying the actions or body language of another person. Con artists use this technique to disarm their victims. It works because it establishes some kind of familiarity that often breaks down defenses.

- As a means of sealing the deal, a scammer is going to flaunt social affiliations because they will make them sound credible. This is similar to companies hiring celebrities to promote their products/brands. Naturally, followers of a famous person will flock towards their idol's endorsement.

- Have you ever got hooked by a limited time offer? You worry about losing the handsome deal, so you scurry to meet the deadline. But shady sales tactics always do this. They show you something too good to miss, and they make it more enticing by giving it a time limit. "This is the last piece", and you worry you may lose your chance so you take the plunge. The worst thing about limited time offer is they work.

- They tease you with things you want to hear because they know that you will want to hear things like, "I can feel a lot of money coming in!" And you believe it or swallow it wholesale because who wouldn't want to see a lot of money coming in. There is nothing more enticing than that.

Con artists are everywhere, and they won't be wearing prison jumpers, so they do not come with a warning. They will come dressed for the part. They look opulent, and they breathe opulence, so they must be the real thing, right?

Is there any need to talk about the Nigerian Emails that everybody seems to know about? They are getting more and more bombastic now than ever before, so how can they tempt anyone? You might think they are stupid, but the ridiculousness is by design. They want responses from only the very gullible so as not to waste time. A Singapore man responded to an email: "I am Winnie Mandela, and I need help to transfer a ton of gold out of the country". It went on to say that 3000 dollars is needed for the freight and his commission is 10 % of several million. After sending the 3000 dollars and the emails stopped coming, he persisted in trying to make contact. Finally, he received an email that said the only way to resolve the matter is for him to go to Nigeria and be brought to the persons concerned. And he did, go to Nigeria, where upon he was taken for ransom. Luckily for him, his family was able to bail him out. When a person wants too much for something to happen, especially when greedy, he can be extremely gullible. Everyone needs to memorize this: If it's too good to be true, it probably is.

Chapter 4: Are You Gullible?

Have you ever been gullible? It doesn't have to be a big thing. It could be a simple April Fools prank or a small-deal investment. If you keep falling for these things over and over again, you need to make a change.

Test: Find Out if You Are Gullible

Before you make changes, you will need to find out for sure, that there is a recurring problem to be remedied.

Go through this checklist and tick the boxes that make sense for you. Every tick stands for a point. Count your scores. If you score more than 11 points or 70% you surely have a problem and you need to make some changes:

☐ Do you know that gullible is not even a real word? It is not in the dictionary. If you considered checking it out in the dictionary, tick this box.

☐ You hide from everyone during April Fool's day because it's safer that way.

☐ You have answered some email scams, thinking you really won an inheritance or something else.

☐ People have called you out more than once for sharing fake news.

☐ You enjoy going to psychics and you gobble up what they say.

- [ ] You believe in star signs and you read your horoscopes daily.

- [ ] You saw the tub of "I can't believe it's not butter", tasted it, and still believe that it's not butter.

- [ ] All good deals are good deals, even those sold in shady places — like gadgets and appliances being sold by strangers from the trunk of their cars.

- [ ] You believe it when people come to you for help, and to extend a hand because they will be truly lost without you.

- [ ] You know that the moon landing didn't happen.

- [ ] You have bought one of those slimming pills.

- [ ] You still believe in Santa Claus and the Tooth Fairy.

- [ ] You have joined a cult.

- [ ] You take several homeopathic remedies.

- [ ] You play the lottery because you know you will win it, one of these days.

Actionable Tips to Correct Your Gullibility

"I had been gullible, naïve, soft, pliable. That's why I got taken advantage of. To survive, you have to have tough skin."
Tia Carrere

1. **Be more analytical.** As already discussed, the automatic response to problems is System 1, which is the fast-thinking, more emotional kind of decision-making process. To protect yourself from scams, cons, and so forth, you need to activate System 2 of thinking which is slower and more analytical. It is a skeptical kind of thinking that chooses to scrutinize the information before accepting it.

2. **Seek to educate yourself.** If you do not want to be the vulnerable one that's always quick to believe anything that's being fed to you, reinforce your understanding by being well-informed. It's easy to trick someone who

doesn't have the facts handy. But when you are well-equipped, no one is going to fool you into believing just about anything. Con men may think twice about trying to dupe you because they know you are going to give them a hard time or to waste their time.

3. **Learn from your past mistakes.** People can fall into traps once, but you shouldn't make a habit of it. Maybe you became a victim of the grandest April Fools prank, once, but you shouldn't take it too hard. Take it as a learning opportunity, so that you do not fall into the cycle, over and over again. There is a saying "You fool me once, shame on you. You fool me twice, shame on me."

4. **Learn how to read and interpret body language.** Subconsciously your body pays attention to people's body language. You need to watch out for the tell-tale signs so that you can uncover their deception before they make a fool out of you. Some signs are out in the open, you just must be more observant and trust your instinct and years of experience. Google "how to read body language".

5. **Study your own patterns.** More than learning for your mistakes, you have to look into your patterns. Study the occasions when you have fallen victim and displayed gullibility and assess the condition you were in, at the moment. Were you distracted? What kind of distraction were you dealing with? Were you stressed? By studying your patterns, you will be able to avoid falling into the traps.

6. **Value your intuition.** There is such a thing as a gut feel. It is a nagging feeling inside of you that tells you that something is wrong. It goes beyond face value because it acknowledges deeper emotions. If you encounter someone or something and it doesn't feel right, pause for a while, to think. Look into what you're feeling and see if there's more to it. Sometimes your intuition functions like a warning light and it will go off if it senses something wrong. You shouldn't ignore it.

7. **Buy yourself some time.** Do not make impulsive decisions, especially big ones. It is best that you buy yourself some time to think about everything. Your understanding and perception may change. Do not make important decisions when you are angry or distracted, such decisions are almost always wrong.

8. **Look for integrity and competence.** Be critical about anyone and anything, if a high stake is involved. No matter how good it looks, sounds and feels, you need to dig deeper. Look for integrity and competence because it will be a better measure.

9. **This was told to the author by a psychiatrist**. He was treating a female patient of her feeling of rage which triggered her depression and sleeplessness, which went on for 10 years. Her anger was fixated towards a man whom she perceived to have gravely wronged her. On further questioning, he found to his amazement, that the man in question had already died more than 10 years ago. Did she not suffer for nothing? Had she not heard of "let bygones be bygones"? Should she not

forgive and forget, and moved on? By the time psychiatrist treatment was necessary it was by then an emotional mental disorder and was handled as such. But what lead on to that? In everyday life there are times when it is gullible to not forgive, forget and move on. By not practicing "bygones be bygones" earlier in her life whenever that was the right thing to do, had gravely affected her emotional and mental health.

10. **In your daily lives.** Last but not least thinking that "It'll not happen to me" can be extremely gullible, especially if health and lives are at stake. This self-proclaim edict is emphatically eclipsed by Murphy's Law that "what can happen will happen". It is only a matter of time. You ride a bicycle long enough, you will fall, only a matter of time. So, isn't it gullible not to take precautions, like slowing down, wearing helmet and knee guards? So too with driving, maybe especially with driving, obviously. Wear seat belt? Drink and drive? "It'll not happen to me".

Be aware that most accidents happen at home. You climb up and down stairs many times a day, Murphy's Law says that you will fall, and many of us have. Safety instructors always tell us to keep one hand on the handrail, a piece of very good advice. Many fatal falls take place in the bathrooms, something to keep in mind. It might not be a bad idea to conduct safety checks in and around the house.

"Don't be gullible, use life before it uses you. Understand there are no free lunches, and for every action you take, there's a reaction."
Sylvester Stallone

Conclusion: We simply cannot resist a Good Story

Fake news is nothing new. Since the beginning of time, the Early Man has huddled around the fire in their caves sharing stories about alien gods, mystical animals and dreams, some of which have been immortalized in cave paintings. When the ancient leader declared war on enemies based on visions appearing in dreams, his people readily believed, even at the risk of losing their lives. Why? Aren't dreams the ultimate fake news? Yet, the idea that the gods have spoken to my king is seductive. This would mean that my king is favored by the gods and therefore I too am on the right side of the gods.

There are lots of gullibility in religions and self-radicalization. The subject is too big for this book, and too controversial to discuss here. In religions, one just have to see the power evangelizing has over some people. In self-radicalization many take place when the victim is at the lowest point of his life. He could be trap in abject poverty with no end in sight. His life is hopeless and the promise of paradise in the after life becomes irresistible. Are suicide bombers super gullible? Or super destitute?

The Good Story captivates and fertilizes our imagination. It fuels our desire, be it power, love or greed, which we all crave for in varying degrees. For this reason, we will always be more gullible than we think. There is no escaping human nature. The rumor that we gleefully spread, is eagerly received by willing ears; it is far more scintillating than the dull truth.

It is this awareness, which I have tried to create with the many examples shown in this book, that is the starting point to avoiding the pitfalls of gullibility, of falling victim to the opportunistic predator or sometimes even to your own prejudiced views.

Healthy skepticism is a good habit to cultivate – ask questions, gather information, check your assumptions- before making decisions about believing what is told to you. Guard though, against becoming conveniently cynical - contemptuous distrust from the onset is merely an excuse not to bother with seeking out the truth. Ironically, the unchecked viewpoint will only plant the seeds to eventual gullibility.

_ *Thank You / Phil Hugh*

P.S. We may be more gullible than we think. Why? If we are not so gullible, the World would be a much happier place. In a world of plenty, we have unnecessary wars and starvation. Whose fault is it?

"If you are emotionally attached to your tribe, religion or political leaning to the point that truth and justice become secondary considerations, your education is useless. Your exposure is useless. If you cannot reason beyond petty sentiments, you are a liability to mankind."
~ Dr. Chuba Okadigbo (Late)

THE END

Go here to check out this other book that might interest you:

Available in Kindle eBook download and in paperback format.

Printed in Great Britain
by Amazon

39933152R00029